A very happy

a.

GW01451335

From the
Abbey
to The
Office

by Dennis Butts

*a short introduction
to Reading and its writers*

First published in the UK in 2008 by
Two Rivers Press
35–39 London Street
Reading RG1 4PS
www.tworiverspress.com

Two Rivers Press is a member of Inpress

Designed by Nadja Guggi
Illustrations by Martin Andrews

Printed and bound by CPI Antony Rowe, Chippenham

Copyright © Dennis Butts 2008
Paddington Bear © Paddington and Company Ltd. 2008

The right of Dennis Butts to be identified as the author
of this work has been asserted by him in accordance
with the Copyright, Design and Patents Act of 1988

ISBN 978-1-901677-59-1

Two Rivers Press gratefully acknowledges
financial assistance from Reading Borough Council.

PREFACE

The historical county town of Reading can boast no world-famous literary figures like Shakespeare, nor has it produced major writers such as Thomas Hardy, the Brontë sisters or William Wordsworth, whose works have become almost synonymous with a particular geographical region, so that we speak of Hardy's Wessex, the Brontë country or Wordsworth's Lakes. Perhaps because of its excellent communications through the centuries by roads, rivers and railways, it seems to have attracted more transitory figures whose connections with Reading seem slighter or less well-known.

Reading is nevertheless the source of Britain's oldest polyphonic song with its world-famous lyrics. It is strongly associated with the beginnings of the English novel. England's most important eighteenth-century poet and greatest nineteenth-century novelist knew Reading, while the later works of Oscar Wilde are closely identified with its Gaol. In modern times Britain's greatest war poet was inspired by staff at Reading's new University College, and in the twenty-first century an ex-pupil of Ashmead School achieved international celebrity by his wit and humour.

This short work does not claim to be a comprehensive history of Reading and all its writers. How could it be? It is merely a modest attempt to draw attention to some of the more interesting writers who were born, educated or lived in Reading, or were associated with it in some significant way. Apologies are offered in advance for any serious errors or omissions.

RELIGION AND CLOTH: 1200–1700

Although Reading is mentioned as the site of one of the great battles
between the kingdom of Wessex and the Vikings in the *Anglo-Saxon
Chronicle* in 871 AD, the earliest imaginative literature associated with
the old town can still be easily seen on a plaque on the ruined wall
of the Chapter House of Reading Abbey:

> Sumer is icumen in
> Lhude sing cuccu!
> Groweth sed and bloweth med,
> And springth the wude nu
> Sing cuccu!

The history of Reading between the years 1121 and 1539, it has been
said, is little more than the history of its great Benedictine Abbey, and
this famous song survives in a manuscript from the Abbey which is now
lodged in the British Library. Although it has been dated about 1260, the
manuscript does present some problems of authorship. One theory holds
that it was written by William de Wycombe, a known medieval composer,
while another suggests that it was owned by a Reading monk, William
of Winchester. Very little seems to be known about him except that on a
visit to Leominster Priory in the 1270s he was brought before the Bishop
of Hereford for 'incontinence' with a number of women including a nun!

Even after King Henry VIII ordered the destruction of Reading Abbey, religion and religious controversy played an immensely important part in the life of the town. The most striking example of this was the career of the sixteenth-century ballad-writer and controversialist William Gray. He might have been a monk, for he had an intimate knowledge of religious houses and seems to have helped Coverdale translate the Bible into English in 1538. The protégé of Thomas Cromwell, he was a ferocious anti-Papist, and between 1535 and 1551 he published a series of ballads attacking Romish practices. Imprisoned in the Fleet for scurrilous feuding, he was released and taken into the King's service. He was able to lease Bulmershe Manor in 1545 and a few years later acquired various lands which had once belonged to the dissolved monastery. Although he was appointed to represent Reading in Parliament in 1547, he was soon in trouble again, and committed to the Tower of London in 1550. But before he died on February 1st 1551, he had been re-instated once more! He may have been buried in Sonning Church, as is his widow, who married Robert Blagrave.

Is there a hidden political or sexual meaning behind Gray's best-known ballad 'The Kinges Hunte is Upp'?

The hunt is up, the hunt is up,
And it is well nigh day;
And Harry our King is gone hunting,
To bring his deer to bay.

The east is bright, with morning light,
And darkness it is fled;
And the merie horne wakes up the morne
To leave his idle bed.

Behold the skyes with golden dyes
Are glowing all around;
The grass is greene, and so are the treen,
All laughing with the sound.

The horses snort to be at sport,
The dogges are running free;
The woddes rejoyce at the mery nois
Of hey tantara tee ree!

The sunne is glad to see us clad
All in our lustie greene,
And smiles in the skye as he riseth hye
To see and to be seen.

Awake all men, I say agen,
Be mery as you maye,
For Harry our King is gone hunting
To bring his deer to bay.

A better-known and even more controversial religious figure was William Laud, who became Archbishop of Canterbury, but was beheaded for treason in 1645. Laud, who was born in Reading in 1573 and lived in a house on the north side of Broad Street, was deeply sensitive throughout his life about his humble origins. He was in fact the son of a master-tailor and thus associated with the cloth trade which had gradually come to rival the importance of the Abbey from its first appearance in the thirteenth century. The wool and cloth trades reached even greater prosperity in the fourteenth and fifteenth centuries, with their clothiers, dyers and weavers, and their powerful Merchants Guild.

THOMAS DELONEY (1543-1600)

The best literary representation of Reading's involvement with the Cloth trade, however, comes not from a Reading man but a silk weaver from Norwich, Thomas Deloney.

Deloney became well-known from the 1580s, particularly for his ballads, but since his death he has become much more highly regarded for two of his late prose works: *The Pleasant History of John Winchcomb, in his younger years called Jack of Newbury* (1597) and *Thomas of Reading: or, the six worthy yeomen* (1600).

Whether Deloney ever visited Reading is not actually known, but in both of these tales he displays a certain amount of local knowledge. *Jack of Newbury* is a rather rambling tale about a prosperous broad-cloth weaver who successfully petitions the king when foreign trade is bad, and has a number of other adventures, lending a draper £500 to get him out of debt, and so on. But there is not much structure here, though the references to Hungerford, Newbury and Wallingford are interesting.

Thomas of Reading is a more considerable piece of work. Unhistorically the story begins in the days of King Henry 1, before the cloth trade was actually established in Reading, although there really was a clothier called Thomas Cole (on whom the story may be based), who lived in the times of King Edward 1 (1272–1307). Thomas and his friends, who are also clothiers, lead prosperous lives, regularly visiting London – so that their wives may buy fine gowns – and feasting the king when he visits them. But tragedy strikes when Thomas is murdered on his way to London at the *Crane Inn* in Colebrook (in a scene which reminds one of *Macbeth*), and his wife has to investigate his disappearance and see that the criminals are caught. The story ends quietly with Thomas's friend, the king, also dying, but asking 'to be buried at Reading, for the great love he bore to that place, among those Clothiers, whose living was his heart's comfort.'

Thomas Deloney is not a great novelist, to be sure, but his two novels – with their realistic stories about merchants and their wives, their servants and maids, their jokes and their feasts – represent one of the earliest attempts to try and depict the everyday life of ordinary people. His works point the way to Fielding and Dickens and the other great novelists.

THE EIGHTEENTH CENTURY:
MANSIONS, SHOPS AND SCHOOLS

Although the woollen industry declined in eighteenth-century Reading, the town survived because its improved roads and waterways provided important trade routes for flour and timber, hardware and coal from all over England. When Daniel Defoe toured Britain in the 1720s he particularly praised Reading's rivers. 'Their chief trade is by this water-navigation to and from London,' he wrote,' though they have necessarily a great trade into the country.'

ALEXANDER POPE (1688–1744)

Alexander Pope was not a Reading man, but his family moved to a small manor house at Binfield in 1700, and the young poet knew Reading through his visits to the Englefield family at Whiteknights, the Stonors at Stonor Park and especially Lyster Blount and his two daughters, Teresa and Martha, at Mapledurham.

Pope was obviously very fond of Berkshire. He wrote about its rural attractions in his pastoral poem 'Windsor Forest' of 1713, and after he left Berkshire he returned to spend a day at his old haunts in 1717, and wrote a Hymn in Windsor Forest, comparing his present problems with his idyllic and inspiring past:

All hail! once pleasing, once inspiring Shade,
Scene of my youthful Loves, and happier hours!
Where the kind Muses met me as I stray'd,
And gently press'd my hand, and said, Be Ours! –
Take all thou ere shal't have, a constant Muse:
At Court thou may'st be lik'd, but nothing gain;
Stock thou may'st buy and sell, but always lose;
And love the brightest eyes, but love in vain.

ALEXANDER POPE (1688–1744)

Pope's reference to 'the brightest eyes' probably refers to his feelings for the Blount sisters, Martha, who was his own age, and Teresa who was two years younger, for he regularly visited them at Mapledurham between 1707 and 1715. Their relationship is problematic, however. Was Pope in love with Teresa – or with both sisters? There are suspicions that two of his most passionate poems, 'Elegy to the Memory of an Unfortunate Lady' and 'Eloisa to Abelard,' are about his unfulfilled love for Teresa, but we do not really know. Pope and Teresa seem to have fallen out in 1718, but the poet remained friendly with Martha, and wrote a noble tribute to her in his 'Epistle to a Lady' of 1733.

By then Pope was living in Twickenham. But he had other Berkshire connections besides the Blount family. In 1711 a feud broke out between the Fermor family of Oxfordshire and the Petre family of Essex. Lord Robert Petre stole a lock of hair from the head of his attractive relative Arabella Fermor, and Pope wrote one of his most charming poems 'The Rape of the Lock' in an attempt to defuse the situation. But this caused even more annoyance, and the fuss did not really die down until Arabella married the Berkshire gentleman Francis Parkins in 1715 and went to live at Ufton Court.

THE BERKSHIRE BALLAD

Another strikingly romantic event which inspired an eighteenth-century poem, is sometimes known as 'The Berkshire Ballad,' or 'The Berkshire Lady's Garland', or, more explicitly, as 'The Sword-Point Wedding.'

This ballad, which first seems to have been published in 1760, tells the story of how a beautiful young heroine met and fell in love with a handsome young gentleman while attending a wedding. Disguising herself with a mask, she challenged him to a duel unless he agreed to marry her. Rather than risk injury, the young bachelor agreed, but when he rode back to her home, she re-appeared to him undisguised in all her beauty, and a happy marriage followed.

Now he's cloth'd in rich attire,
Not inferior to a squire;
Beauty, honour, riches, store!
What can man desire more?

What makes the ballad even more remarkable is that it seems to have
been based upon a real event, the courtship of the Reading heiress Frances
Kendrick, who grew up in Whitley Park, and Benjamin Child, a young
lawyer from Oxford. Frances and Benjamin married at St. Mary's Church,
Wargrave, in 1707.

JOHN NEWBERY (1713–1767)

As trade developed in the eighteenth century, the town started expanding,
and there were many markets and fairs. William Carnan ran a bookshop
at the 'Bible and Crown' in Market Place, and also printed the *Reading
Mercury* newspaper. John Newbery, the son of a farmer at Waltham
St. Lawrence, became his assistant. When Carnan died in 1737, Newbery
married his widow, who was about six years older than him, and had been
left with three children. He took over the business, and, as well as selling
patent medicines, began to specialise even more in books, newspapers and
periodicals. Then about 1744 Newbery moved to London, and opened
a shop near the Chapter House in St. Paul's Churchyard.

From now on Newbery's career really took off. While continuing to
sell other items, such as 'Dr. James' celebrated Fever Powder,' Newbery
concentrated more, not only on selling books, but commissioning and
publishing them. His masterstroke was to realise, as perhaps nobody
earlier had understood, that the rising and ambitious middle classes were
looking for books not only to educate but also to entertain their children.

In 1744 Newbery published a landmark volume – *A Little Pretty
Pocket Book* – specifically for the amusement of young children, priced
at sixpence for the book alone, but eightpence with a ball for boys or a

pin-cushion for girls. Newbery's business flourished, and, though he also produced books for adults, often employing such authors as Christopher Smart and Oliver Goldsmith, he is world-famous for being the first publisher to publish large numbers of entertaining books for children, such as the celebrated *Goody Two Shoes* of 1765. John Newbery is buried in the churchyard at Waltham St. Lawrence, and there is a brilliant account of him by Dr. Johnson as 'Jack Whirler' in the Idler magazine in 1758.

After Newbery's death the London business was carried on by his son Francis and stepson Thomas Carnan, while the bookshop in Reading continued at the 'Bible and Crown'. After the death of Christopher Smart in 1771, Newbery gave employment to Smart's widow (Newbery's stepdaughter Anna Carnan) and daughter Elizabeth back in Reading. In 1795 Elizabeth married Jean Baptist Le Noire de la Brosse, a French emigré who had settled in Reading, and she started writing, publishing the novel *Village Annals* in 1803 and her *Miscellaneous Poems* in 1825. Eventually the bookshop, after various changes, was bought by George Lovejoy who moved to London Street in 1832.

HYMN WRITERS AND PREACHERS

Not surprisingly, given the presence of so many churches from the twelfth century – the Abbey, St. Mary's, Greyfriars, St. Laurence's – and with the arrival of non-conformists from the seventeenth century, Reading has always witnessed a fair amount of religious literature. The eighteenth century in particular produced numerous preachers and theologians, such as Dr. Robert South (1633–1716), the Rev. William Bennett (1765–1796) and Dr. W. Talbot (1717–1794). Two writers deserve special mention, however, James Merrick (1720–1769) and John Cennick (1718–1755).

James Merrick, the son of a physician, was educated at Reading School and Trinity College, Oxford, and went on to become a prolific scholar and poet. He wrote many hymns but is best known for his translation of *The Psalms of David* in 1765. John Cennick, on the other hand, had a much more erratic career. The grandson of a clothier, he worked as a carpenter and then as a land-surveyor, but around 1738 was invited by the Wesley brothers to become a teacher at their new school for colliers' children at Kingswood. After some religious disagreements, however, he left in 1740 and moved to London, where he became a successful preacher for the Moravian Church. Among many hymns he wrote, the best known is one revised by the Wesleys which begins 'Lo, He comes with clouds descending ... '

JANE AUSTEN (1770–1817)

SCHOOLS

Reading School was founded in the Middle Ages but had experienced many vicissitudes before being successfully revived in the late eighteenth century by Dr. Richard Valpy (1754–1836), who was Headmaster from 1781 to 1830. A dynamic figure in many ways, he wrote numerous school textbooks and produced various editions of Shakespeare's plays, but he also published a collection of his own poems – *Poetical Blossoms, or a collection of poems, odes and translations* in 1772.

The other important school at the end of the eighteenth century was the Abbey School, a boarding-school run by emigrés, which occupied rooms over the Abbey Gateway and overflowed into the adjoining house. Jane Austen (1770–1817) was at the Abbey Gate with her older sister Cassandra from 1785–1786. (There may even be a brief reference in the description of Mrs. Goddard's school in *Emma* of 1816.) Mrs. Sherwood (1775–1851), who became one of England's most influential children's writers in the nineteenth century was also a pupil at the school from the age of sixteen to eighteen. She left, we are told, with a considerable degree of social polish and a good knowledge of elegant conversational French. Mrs. Sherwood's most famous book *The History of the Fairchild Family* (1818, 1842 and 1847) contains what looks like a fairly accurate and sympathetic account of the Abbey School; and when the Fairchild family come into unexpected wealth they go to live in a grand house at Reading called 'The Grove'.

THE NINETEENTH CENTURY:
RAILWAYS, ELECTIONS AND PUBLIC BUILDINGS

Although the population of Reading had risen steadily from around 4,700 in 1600 to over 9,000 in 1801, before the arrival of the railway in 1840 it still had all the characteristics of a small English county town. William Cobbett, who visited it in November 1822 particularly praised its citizens: 'I am delighted with the people that I have seen at Reading,' he wrote. 'Their kindness to me is nothing in my estimation compared with the sense and spirit which they appear to express.'

MARY RUSSELL MITFORD (1787–1855)

Nobody captured the ethos and spirit of pre-industrial Berkshire and Reading more than Mary Russell Mitford. Although born in Hampshire, the daughter of a feckless medical doctor, the family first moved to Reading in 1791 when Mary was four years old. But Dr. Mitford's high living and extravagance saw him squander his wife's fortune, and the family moved away for a time. In 1797 young Mary won £20,000 on an Irish Lottery, however, and the family moved back to Reading to 39 London Road, although Mary was actually educated at the Abbey School when it transferred to London. Eventually Dr. Mitford bought and re-built Grazeley Court, a large house (re-named Bertram House) on the outskirts of Reading, mainly with the proceeds of Mary's winnings. Mary saw a good deal of Reading society at this time, and attended many local balls and even Reading races. But Dr. Mitford's gambling habits gradually led to his downfall, and the family had to sell Bertram House and move to a small cottage at Three Mile Cross in 1819. By now, however, Mary had begun to achieve some reputation as a poet, and in the 1820s had several plays successfully produced, such as *Julian* (1823) and *Rienzi* (1828).

During these years Mary was also regularly contributing articles and sketches to such periodicals as the *Ladies Magazine* and *New Monthly Magazine*, and these were eventually collected together and published in separate volumes under the title of *Our Village* from 1824–1832. They were a great success, frequently reprinted, and established Mary Mitford as an important literary figure.

Our Village consists of a series of sketches and short stories about country life and society focusing on an imaginary village. There are short, mainly descriptive essays, such as 'Frost and Thaw' and 'The First Primrose,' mixed in with amusing stories, such as an account of a village cricket-match, and sad ones such as the story of some boys who were drowned in a chalk-pit. The tales are full of realistic observations of local people – farmers, landlords, servants, soldiers, and even mole-catchers. There are many, largely happy, love affairs and marriages. A young gypsy girl marries the game-keeper, and Colonel Sandford happily weds his young ward. Although there is little social analysis here at a time when there was considerable rural distress, there is a sense of the business of ordinary lives, and much more about poverty and hardship – among widows, gypsies and poor soldiers – than Mary Mitford is normally given credit for. But there is also a warmth and humour that reminds one of Mrs. Gaskell's *Cranford*.

Belford Regis (1835) is a collection of sketches and tales about the country town called Belford Regis (i.e. Reading). Elizabeth Barrett Browning regarded it as Mary Mitford's best work – and indeed it is more dramatic, with fewer purely descriptive entries than *Our Village*. The work focuses upon the inhabitants of Belford Regis as they were perhaps at the

MARY RUSSELL MITFORD (1787–1855)

beginning of the nineteenth century. The Napoleonic Wars are in the background and the Enclosure Movement is causing some distress, as we follow the lives of shop-keepers, priests, business men, local aristocrats, carpenters and Members of Parliament. Although Reform is in the air, we are really getting a picture of Reading as it was thirty years earlier, with the different stories linked together by the recurring presence of a few central characters – Stephen Lane, the butcher, Louis Duval, an artist, and the Rev. Singleton.

By the 1830s Mary Mitford had become a celebrated figure, the friend of Wordsworth and Robert Browning, but with failing health. Her father, whom she had supported by her literary earnings, died in 1842, leaving her with many debts. Her last important work was her *Recollections of a Literary Life* (1852). The poor state of her cottage led her to move to Swallowfield in 1851, and here she died in January 1855.

One of Mary Mitford's literary acquaintances at the beginning of the nineteenth century, Mrs. Barbara Hofland (1770–1844) also had strong connections with Reading, for her husband, T. C. Hofland, the landscape artist, was commissioned by the Marquis of Blandford to produce a book containing illustrations celebrating his mansion at Whiteknights. Barbara, who wrote a long descriptive poem to accompany the illustrations, became a good friend of Mary's during her regular visits to Reading, but by the time *A Descriptive Account of Whiteknights* was finished in 1819, the Marquis, now Duke of Marlborough, was virtually bankrupt, and the Hoflands did not receive a penny for their labours.

Other nineteenth-century writers included Henry Hart Milman (1791–1868), one-time Vicar of St. Mary's, who achieved considerable success with such religious dramas as *The Fall of Jerusalem* (1820) and *The Martyr of Antioch* (1822). The brothers Walter White (1811–1893) and William White (1820–1900) were well-known for their travel-books, and William Deacon (1799–1844) achieved great popularity with *Warreniana* (1824), his comic parodies of such writers as Byron and Wordsworth, which rapidly went into four editions in so many years. Although primarily a historian, John Man (1749–1824) is remembered for his sprightly series of letters about Reading purporting to be from a traveller to his friend in London, first published in 1810 under the title of *The Stranger in Reading*. A later writer, Mortimer Collins (1827–1876), was already a well-known poet and novelist, author of such books as *Sweet Anne Page* (1868), when he moved to Knowl Hill on his second marriage in 1868. One of Mary Mitford's best Reading friends, however, was the lawyer and author Thomas Noon Talfourd.

THOMAS NOON TALFOURD (1795–1854)
Thomas Noon Talfourd was born in Reading and attended various schools before studying at Reading School under Dr. Valpy. At the age of sixteen he published his first volume of poems and continued to contribute to journals and magazines while studying law in London. He was called to

the Bar in 1821, and became friendly with such writers as Charles Lamb and Samuel Taylor Coleridge. In 1835 he was elected MP for Reading and made a major contribution in Parliament by introducing a Copyright Bill, to protect the rights of authors, which eventually became law in 1842. Created a serjeant-at-law in 1835, he became a judge in 1845, and actually died in Court at Stafford, while carrying out his legal duties in 1854.

Although he regularly contributed to magazines, and even had a farce *Freemasonry: or, More Secrets than One* produced in the Old Theatre in Friar Street in 1815, Talfourd's major literary successes came from several plays in the 1830s, *Ion* (1835), *The Athenian Captive* (1837) and *Glencoe; or, the Fate of the MacDonalds* in 1839. *Ion*, a quasi-Greek tragedy about King Ion's self-sacrifice in order to overcome a great pestilence, is the best of them, and enjoyed considerable success when produced at Covent Garden, but these works seem unlikely to excite much interest today. Talfourd's *Letters and Life of Charles Lamb* (1839) has lasted, however, with its fascinating and warm-hearted account of a writer Talfourd knew well. One of Charles Lamb's greatest friends was his old school-fellow Samuel Taylor Coleridge, and the great romantic poet and critic had an extraordinary connection with Reading.

SAMUEL TAYLOR COLERIDGE (1772–1834)

Samuel Taylor Coleridge, the great poet and critic, must have been desperate when he came to Reading in 1793. A young student at Cambridge, Coleridge was hard pressed by debts and other problems in the autumn of 1793, so he abandoned the University and volunteered to join the army as a private in the 15th Light Dragoons. Sworn in at the regimental headquarters in Reading, he was equipped with leather breeches, stable jacket, riding boots and a carbine, and began his military career mucking out the stables. He gave a false name, using his initials, as Silas Tomkyn Comberbache.

After two months training, during which he did guard duty at Reading Fair, he was seconded to Henley, where his main job was to nurse a fellow-soldier who had smallpox. But news of his whereabouts eventually reached Cambridge. In some accounts, Coleridge gave himself away by correcting a Greek quotation made by an officer; in another account, he revealed his identity by telling stories of the Peloponnesian War; in a third version, he pencilled lines from a Latin poem over his harness-peg. Whatever the truth, Coleridge's friends rallied round and arranged his release from the army. After a payment of twenty-five guineas, he was finally discharged in April 1794. The Regimental Roll read: 'discharged S. T. Comberbache, Insane, 10 April, 1794.'

CHARLES DICKENS (1812–1870)

But Talfourd also knew most of the major writers of his day, most importantly Charles Dickens. They probably first met around 1837 when Talfourd was introducing his Copyright Bill into Parliament. Copyright was an issue Dickens felt very strongly about, so it is not surprising that Dickens dedicated *Pickwick Papers* to Talfourd when it was first published in 1837. It helped to establish the important link between Charles Dickens and Reading.

In 1841 Talfourd decided not to stand for re-election as a Reading MP, perhaps fearing a Tory victory, so the Liberal Party were on the lookout for another candidate. George Lovejoy (1808–1883), the London Street bookseller, was the local Liberal Party agent and, perhaps following up a suggestion from Talfourd, wrote to Dickens, inviting him to stand as a Reading MP. Though flattered by the invitation, Dickens declined, pleading that he could not afford the expense of a contested election. His decision was probably the right one, and two Conservative candidates were returned for Reading in 1841. But Dickens's courteous rejection inevitably raises the intriguing speculation – 'What if ... '

Dickens remained in touch with Reading, however. In 1843, when the Mechanics' Institution, renamed the Literary, Scientific and Mechanics' Institution, re-opened in new buildings in London Street – today re-named *Great Expectations* – Lovejoy invited Dickens to its inaugural

SAMUEL TAYLOR COLERIDGE (1772–1834)

CHARLES DICKENS (1812–1870)

dinner in October, and Dickens wrote to apologise for his absence. Talfourd did attend and speak however, referring to one 'whose genius was as universal as the nature he illustrated … Charles Dickens.'

But in 1851 Dickens did come to Reading. Earlier in the year he had founded the Guild of Literature and Art, mainly to help impoverished writers; and in order to raise funds for this Dickens and his friends put on theatrical performances in various parts of the country. The Mayor of Reading, William Darter, invited Dickens to Reading. Thus it came about that on 23 December Dickens and his company came to Reading's

Town Hall and played two comedies – Bulwer Lytton's *Not So Bad as We Seem* and *Mr. Nightingale's Diary* by Dickens and Mark Lemon. The evening was a great success and the *Reading Mercury* reported that the 400 present expressed their 'unqualified delight.'

When Talfourd died in March 1854, Dickens wrote at once to express his sympathy to Talfourd's widow. Talfourd had been the President of the Literary, Scientific and Mechanics' Institution, and Dickens was honoured to accept the invitation to take over his friend's office on 27 March, forwarding at the same time his subscription for a life-membership. By this time in his career Dickens had begun giving public readings of his works, and on 19 December he came to Reading to give his reading of *A Christmas Carol*. Before he began, he paid tribute to Talfourd for 'his noble nature and his simple heart,' and, at the end of the performance, the *Reading Mercury* reported that the audience responded so enthusiastically to Dickens that 'this demonstration of feeling seemed, for a moment, to overcome him.'

So ended Dickens's association with Reading – except, that is, for a curious footnote. Esther Summerson, the heroine of Dickens's great novel *Bleak House* (1853), is brought up in Windsor, but when her godmother dies, she is taken to be educated at the Greenleaf Boarding School in Reading run by the two Miss Donny sisters. But what made Dickens think of Reading just then? He had begun to have his first ideas about writing *Bleak House* in February 1851, and visited Reading later that year. Was it this visit that suggested the place for his heroine's schooling?

ARTHUR RIMBAUD (1854–1891)

A few years after Dickens's death, the great French poet Arthur Rimbaud came to London in the spring of 1874, hoping to find a job. After travelling around Britain, he finally obtained a post teaching French in Reading, and apparently worked at 165 Kings Road from August onwards. But he soon tired of it, and in November inserted an advertisement in the *Times* newspaper for a post offering an opportunity to travel 'in southern and eastern countries.' He left Reading and for the next few years drifted around Europe, Africa and the Far East, including Indonesia, Cyprus and Ethiopia, although he managed to publish his masterpiece *Les Illuminations* in 1886. He died in Marseilles at the age of thirty-seven.

OSCAR WILDE (1854–1900)

With the coming of the railways in the 1840s new buildings began to spring up in Victorian Reading, with the Royal Berkshire Hospital in 1839, the Station in 1840, and the arrival of Huntley and Palmers in 1841. Among these developments was the building of Reading Gaol in 1842– 1844, and this was to become the harsh if temporary home of one of the most famous writers associated with Reading.

Oscar Wilde, the Irish-born poet, essayist, novelist and playright, enjoyed a dazzling career in London in the second half of the nineteenth century with such plays as *Lady Windermere's Fan* of 1893. But in 1895 he was charged with gross indecency and sentenced to two years' hard labour. He was transferred to Reading Gaol on 21 November, being jeered by spectators at Clapham Junction on the way. On arrival at Reading he was placed in Cell 3.3. Although treated with some sympathy, for he was allowed to work in the prison garden and library, and visited by his wife and friends, his health deteriorated rapidly, and, although he petitioned for his release in June 1896, nothing came of his request.

While in Reading prison he wrote one of his greatest prose works, a long letter to his friend Lord Alfred Douglas, later entitled *De Profundis* (1905), in which he tried to justify his life. But Wilde was also deeply affected by the sufferings of his fellow-prisoners, as we know from the record Thomas Martin, a friendly warder, kept of Oscar Wilde's last months in gaol. Wilde was angered when a half-witted inmate was sentenced to twenty-four lashes, and when three young children were imprisoned for snaring rabbits. (Thomas Martin seems to have been dismissed from the service for giving the smallest child a biscuit.)

OSCAR WILDE (1854–1900)

Oscar Wilde was also deeply moved when Charles Thomas Wooldridge, a trooper in the Royal Horse Guards, was hanged in July 1896 for murdering his wife. When Wilde was released from prison on 18 May 1897, he was taken in a cab to Twyford station, and left England for Dieppe, where he wrote a long letter to the *Daily Chronicle* about the treatment of children in prison. Later in July he started writing his most famous poem the *Ballad of Reading Gaol*, and by August it was virtually finished. Published in February 1898 under the author's name of C 3.3., it reached a sixth impression by May, but it was not until a seventh printing in June 1899 that Oscar Wilde inserted his own name in brackets beside C 3.3. on the title-page. Wilde found in the realities of his prison experiences, the account of a murderer's execution, the inspiration for the most powerful and moving poem he ever wrote:

In Reading gaol by Reading town
There is a pit of shame,
And in it lies a wretched man
Eaten by teeth of flame,
In a burning winding-sheet he lies,
And his grave has got no name.

And there, till Christ call forth the dead,
In silence let him lie:
No need to waste the foolish tear,
Or heave the windy sigh:
The man had killed the thing he loved,
And so he had to die.

And all men kill the things they love,
By all let all this be heard,
Some do it with a bitter look,
Some with flattering word,
The coward does it with a kiss,
The brave man with a sword!

It is appropriate that Reading has commemorated Wilde's genius by naming the avenue between the walls of the Gaol and the river Kennet in his memory.

THE COMING OF THE UNIVERSITY

From the nineteenth century, many adults were thirsting for education in Reading as the success of the Literary Institution and then the beginning of Extension Lectures in 1885 showed. In 1892 a University Extension College was founded, which in 1904 was given, as Reading University College, a new site in London Road with Dr. W.M. Childs (1869–1939) as Principal. One of its earliest appointments was an English lecturer Edith Morley (1875–1964), and she played a crucial part in the career of one of Britain's finest poets, Wilfred Owen.

WILFRED OWEN (1893–1918)

Wilfred Owen came from Shropshire, and after leaving school was uncertain of his vocation. Although he wanted to write, he also considered the possibility of the Church. In 1911 he came to Dunsden as an unpaid lay-assistant and pupil at the vicarage of the Rev. Hubert Wigan. His main work was assisting at services, visiting the poor of the village, and taking Sunday School, but he also found time to write poetry.

Owen was ambitious, and on 29 February 1911, he cycled into Reading for an interview with Dr. Childs, Principal of the University College. Owen wanted to sit for the Intermediate Arts degree in English, Latin, Botany, French and History the following year. He also arranged to attend some Botany classes for six hours a week. When his Botany

WILFRED OWEN (1893–1918)

lecturer discovered that Owen's main interest was in literature, however, she sent him to the Head of the English Department, Miss Morley, who found him, she said, an 'unhappy adolescent, suffering badly from lack of understanding....and in need of encouragement and praise.' These she evidently gave him, together with some advice about the technicalities of poetry, and she suggested that he should read Ruskin and Milton on his free afternoons. She urged him to sit for a scholarship to the University College, and invited him to attend her remaining classes in Old English free of charge.

After his summer holiday in Scotland, Owen returned to Dunsden and continued writing poetry. But he was increasingly unhappy there. He began to lose his Christian faith and in February 1913 left Dunsden. Later in the year he did try to win a scholarship to Reading University College but failed, and in September he left England for a teaching post in Bordeaux.

The rest, as they say, is history. In 1915 Owen enlisted in the army, and, as a result of his experiences at the front, wrote some of our greatest war poetry, before his death on 4 November 1918. It is a rich and tragic story, but one in which Reading played a small but significant part.

While at Dunsden Owen assisted at the double funeral of a mother and her four year-old daughter. Here are some lines from the poem (untitled) he wrote about it:

Deep under turfy grass and heavy clay
They laid her bruised body, and the child.
Poor victims of a swift mischance were they,
Adown Death's trapdoor suddenly beguiled.
I, weeping not, as others, but heart-wild,
Affirmed to Heaven that even Love's fierce flame
Must fail beneath the chill of this cold shame.

So I rebelled, scorning and mocking such
As had the ignorant callousness to wed
On altar steps long frozen by the touch
Of stretcher after stretcher of our dead.
Love's blindness is so terrible, I said;
I will go counsel men, and show what bin
The harvest of their loves is gathered in.

ROBERT GIBBINGS (1889–1958)

Although Elspeth Huxley (1907–1997) studied Agriculture at the University in the 1920s and later became famous for such autobiographical novels as *The Flame Trees of Thika* (1954), Robert Gibbings, the distinguished author, printer, engraver and sculptor, is the other major literary figure associated with Reading University in the first half of the twentieth century.

Gibbings was already famous from the 1920s, because of his own engravings and illustrations but also because of his management of the world-renowned Golden Cockerel Press, which published beautifully printed editions of such works as *The Four Gospels* at Waltham St. Lawrence. Gibbings was forced for financial reasons, however, to sell the Press in 1933. But this was the same year that Anthony Betts was appointed Head of the Art School at what since 1926 had become Reading University. Betts was anxious to recruits high-quality staff to his Department, and in 1936 he recruited Gibbings as 'Sessional Lecturer in Typography, Book Production and Engraving'. (The pay was £3 per day.) Gibbings became a full-time Lecturer in 1937, and, while continuing to publish limited-edition books, also found time to write such books as *Blue Angels and Whales* in 1938. (One cannot help wondering whether Gibbings might not have met the young poet Laurie Lee (1914–1997) at this time, for in 1936, after returning from Spain, Lee lived at Padworth and then 80 London Road, while enrolled as a part-time student in the Art Department of the University, but in September 1937 Lee returned to Spain.)

In 1939 Gibbings had the idea of building a boat with which he rowed down the river Thames during that summer. The journey was interrupted by the outbreak of war. (His family was evacuated to Canada and Gibbings himself moved into St. Patrick's Hall.) But Gibbings completed his journey the following year and his account, illustrated by his own engravings, achieved a great success when published as *Sweet Thames Run Softly* in November 1940. His charming semi-autobiography, semi-travel book, crammed with incidents and humour, sold over 100,000 copies by 1956.

Stimulated by this success, Gibbings went on to enjoy similar adventures, publishing such books as *Coming Down the Wye* in 1942, *Lovely is the Lee* in 1944, and *Coming Down the Seine* in 1953. Gibbings became so successful, in fact, that he was able to resign from the University in late 1942 in order to concentrate upon his own works. He died in 1958, having completed his last work *Till I End My Song* a year earlier.

ROBERT GIBBINGS (1889–1958)

POST-WAR DEVELOPMENTS AT THE UNIVERSITY

In 1946 the University appointed Frank Stenton (1880–1967), Professor of Modern History since 1912, as its Vice-Chancellor. The University was still small in size with only 793 undergraduates, but it was beginning to think of expanding, for in that same year it acquired a new site at Whiteknights, once the estate of the Marquis of Blandford. From now on University appointments often included members of staff who were able to combine writing with their academic work.

Probably the best-known of these in the immediate post-war years was John Wain (1925–1994), poet, novelist and critic, who taught in the English Department from 1947–1955, and became famous for such novels as *Hurry On Down* (1953). Professor Betts encouraged Wain to publish his poems *Mixed Feelings* (Reading School of Art, 1951), and it was no doubt through Wain's friendship with Kingsley Amis that the School of Art also published Amis's poetry collection *A Frame of Mind* in 1953. Other Departments in the University boasted famous writers, too. Michael Hamburger (1924–2004), the distinguished poet, critic and translator, worked in the German Department from 1955–1964. Professor Luigi Meneghello (1922–2007), who had first come to Reading in the 1940s and became Professor in the Italian Department in 1964, achieved a world-wide reputation for such books as *Libera nos a malo* (1963), with their extraordinary mixture of fiction and autobiography, philology and folklore. Marion Lomax (b.1953), now known as Robyn Bolam, who worked in the University Library from 1976–1978, has gone on to achieve a reputation as a poet for such books as *The Peepshow Girl* (1989).

The University's interest in publishing became even more active in the 1970s when Ian Fletcher (1920–1988), from the English Department, and himself a noted poet, combined with Michael Twyman (b.1934) from the Department of Typography to produce an interesting series of publications, chosen by Fletcher and designed by students of Typography, under the name of the Whiteknights Press. Over a dozen pamphlets have been published so far and not all of them have Reading connections, but two deserve special mention: *Floodsheaf* (1974), a collection of poems by Christopher Salvesen (b.1935), and the *War Poems* (1990) of Geoffrey Matthews (1920–1984). Both authors were long-standing members of the English Department. Another important publication of the Whiteknights Press is *Beckett at Reading* (1998), the catalogue of the important collection of manuscripts by the great Irish dramatist and writer, Samuel Beckett, which are held by the University. Jim Knowlson (Emeritus Professor of French) is the author of the definitive biography of Beckett entitled *Damned to Fame* (1996).

During recent years the University has also employed from time to time professional writers to help more informally on the campus by encouraging students' writing and running creative writing seminars, for example. John McGahern (1934–2006), the Irish novelist, the poets Richard Murphy (b.1927), and Peter Porter (b.1929), the American fantasy writer Ursula Le Guin (b.1929), and most recently the outstanding children's writer Philip Pullman (b.1946), author of the trilogy *His Dark Materials*, have all worked in Reading in this capacity. Woodley's teacher-training institution Bulmershe College (now part of the University) also engaged a number of writers-in-residence including the novelist Philip Callow (1924–2007), the dramatist Ted Whitehead (b.1933), the poets Anne Stevenson (b.1933) and Patricia Beer (1924–1994), and the local Reading novelist Sue Krisman.

The University's connection with imaginative writers continues to the present, for it boasts the novelists Gillian Freeman (b. 1929) and Peter Lovesey (b. 1936) among its graduates, and in 2007 appointed the British poet Peter Robinson (b. 1953), author of *This Other Life* (1988) and other works as Professor of English and American Literature.

THE TOWN, POST-WAR AND TODAY

With the arrival of the seed merchants Suttons, the success of Huntley and Palmer's biscuit-factory and the growth of other industries such as brewing Victorian Reading continued to expand with the population rising from just over 21,000 in 1851 to 72,000 in 1901. That growth continued through the twentieth century with the population reaching 143,000 in 2001. The character of the town inevitably changed as the result of two world wars, the impact of new technologies – motorways, computers, supermarkets – and all the advantages and disadvantages of global capitalism. Those changes at first were gradual, however, and perhaps until the middle of the twentieth century Reading was still recognisable as a successful county town, some of whose features were captured in the novels of Elizabeth Taylor.

ELIZABETH TAYLOR (1912–1975)

Elizabeth Taylor, the popular novelist and short-story writer, was undoubtedly the most important Reading-born writer of the twentieth century. Born Elizabeth Coles, she was educated at the Abbey School where she began writing, often secretly. She worked as a governess among other jobs, but after her marriage to a businessman in 1936, she moved to Penn in Buckinghamshire and published her first novel *At Mrs. Lippincote's* in 1945. This is a story about a young married woman's small domestic crises during war-time, and with its references to the river, the Abbey ruins, and the prison it looks as if it is set in Reading. A later novel *Angel* (1957) tells the story of the rise and fall of a bad but incredibly successful popular novelist, rather like 'Marie Corelli,' and the heroine's town of Norley again looks remarkably like Reading with a town square called the Butts, a canal by the brewery, and a prison near a park 'where there was a great cast-iron statue of a lion.'

The author of a dozen novels and four volumes of short stories, Elizabeth Taylor wrote mainly about the lives of the middle and upper classes with a subtlety and humour which has sometimes been compared to Jane Austen. But the short stories, such as 'The Thames Spread Out' and 'The Benefactress,' show her at her best, when she seems able to combine greater powers of pathos, even tragedy, with her characteristically sharp observation and humour.

ELIZABETH TAYLOR (1912–1975)

Leighton Park School is another of Reading's schools which has produced a number of twentieth-century writers. Basil Bunting (1900– 1985) is now regarded as a major modern poet for such works as *Briggflatts* (1966), while the poet Nicholas Moore (1918–1986) was a prominent member of the Apocalyptic Movement in the 1940s, best known for *The Glass Tower* of 1944.

Sue Krisman and Leslie Wilson (b.1952) are two Reading authors who have made reputations as novelists, Sue for such novels as *Ducks and Drakes* (1981) and Leslie for *The Mountain of Immoderate Desires* (1997). Leslie has also produced an outstanding children's book *Last Train to Kummersdorf* (2004). Chris Freddi (b.1955), formerly of Reading School, published his first novel *Pelican Blood* in 2005, while Jane Wight has privately published a number of selections of verse and prose such as *Catching the Sun* (1984). The engaging performance poet A. F. Harrold (b.1975), who studied Philosophy at the University in the 1990s, regularly advances the cause of literature with monthly readings at the Poets' Café in South Street. Last but not least, we should not forget Reading's own Two Rivers Press, which was founded in 1994, and publishes local authors (Adam Sowan: *A Much-maligned Town*, 2008) and local poets (Jane Draycott: *Tideway*, 2002).

RICKY GERVAIS

The most remarkable and successful Reading writer of the twenty-first century is, however, the former Ashmead student Ricky Gervais. Born in 1961, Ricky Gervais grew up in Whitley Wood and after school, studied Biology and then Philosophy at University College, London. He began his career in the world of pop music and recording, before taking various jobs in broadcasting.

From July 2001, however, with his friend Stephen Merchant he created an extraordinary television series called *The Office*. This at first baffling programme seemed to be a documentary about office life in a large company in the Thames Valley, but one which quite baldly revealed the sometimes quite crude ethos and personal relationships within the office. Gradually the viewer learned to appreciate the sharp observation and acute writing behind this deliberately-constructed mock-documentary, in which broad humour, subtle wit and moral satire, for example, at the exposure of hypocrisy, combined to create a rich comedy of social embarrassment.

Here is David Brent (brilliantly played by Ricky Gervais), the Office Manager, talking directly to the camera to show himself a caring employer:

'What is the single most important thing for a company? Is it the building? Is it the stock? Is it the turnover? It's the people. Investment in people. My proudest moment here wasn't when I increased profits by seventeen per cent, or cut expenditure without losing a single member of staff. No. It was a young Greek guy, first job in the country, hardly spoke a word of English, but he came to me and he went, "Mr. Brent will you be the Godfather to my child?"
(HE NODS, SMUGLY. BEAT.)
Didn't happen in the end. We had to let him go, he was rubbish.
He was rubbish.

After a slow start, the three series of *The Office* in 2001, 2002 and 2003 were spectacularly successful, not only reaching large TV audiences but winning BAFTA Awards for the best situation somedies in 2002, 2003 and 2004, and American Emmy Awards for 2005 and 2006. An entirely different comedy series *Extras* in 2005 was almost as popular. Gervais's success is not only the result of good acting and direction but also acute characterisation.

CHILDREN'S WRITERS

Children's literature has always had strong connections with Reading, beginning with the pioneering figure of John Newbery in the eighteenth century, and Mrs. Sherwood in the first half of the nineteenth century.

William Gordon Stables (1840–1910) is Reading's best-known Victorian children's writer. Born in Scotland, he became a naval surgeon and travelled all over the world until he was invalided home. He settled at Twyford in the 1870s and set himself up at Ruscombe House as a journalist, adviser on family health and expert on the care of animals. For many years he toured Britain in a luxurious horse-drawn caravan which he called his land-yacht, equipped with his violin, Spanish guitar, Royal Navy sword and a revolver. (He also took with him his Newfoundland dog and a grey parrot.) But he was most famous for his writing for boys, especially his adventure stories, such as *The Cruise of the Snowbird* (1882) and *For England, Home and Beauty* (1891), which were often serialised in the *Boy's Own Paper*. Stables seems to have lived the life of a glorious eccentric, and is buried in Ruscombe churchyard.

Two writers associated with Reading University also made significant contributions to children's literature: Allen W. Seaby (1867–1953) and Kathleen Hale (1898–2000). Seaby trained as a teacher before studying art at Reading where he became Professor of Fine Art from 1920–1933. He had a distinguished career as a painter and woodcut artist, but his

children's books, such as *Skewbald the New Forest Pony*, first published in 1923, with Seaby's delicate black-and-white sketches, have enjoyed a lasting popularity. Kathleen Hale, who actually studied under Seaby from 1915–1917, is even better known. In 1938 she wrote and illustrated *Orlando the Marmalade Cat* for her two sons, and this became the first of a widely-acclaimed series of entertaining books, which, with their lavish and brightly-coloured lithographic illustrations, have become world-famous.

Another extremely popular author of children's fantasies is Michael Bond (b.1926). Although born in Newbury, he grew up in Reading, living at 21 Gloucester Road – and supporting the local football team at Elm Park – when his father worked for the Post Office. After the end of World War II, Bond combined working for the BBC with writing, and, when he published *A Bear called Paddington* in 1958, he began an enormously popular series of books about the amusing adventures of a small bear, who was named after the railway station familiar to all who travel by train from Reading to London.

Cynthia Harnett (1893–1981), who lived near Sonning Common, is one of Britain's best known writers of historical novels for children, producing well-researched and engaging stories such as *The Wool Pack* (1951) and *The Load of Unicorn* (1959). *The Wool Pack* won the Carnegie Medal for an outstanding children's book in 1951. In 1997 Melvin Burgess (b. 1954), who had been a pupil at Maiden Erlegh School, also won the Carnegie Medal for his book *Junk*. Burgess writes challenging and even disturbing books for young adults, and *Junk* documents the attractions and dangers of drug-addiction. A later work *Doing* (2003) attracted even more controversy for its disturbing account of adolescent sexual *mores*.

VISITORS

Daniel Defoe and William Cobbett are only two writers among many who have paid brief visits to Reading. The strangest was perhaps Stephen Duck (1705–1756), the eighteenth-century peasant-poet. A Wiltshire man, Stephen made an early reputation with his poem *The Thresher's Labour* of 1730 which offered a vivid account of a farm-worker's life. His later work was less successful, however, although he gained the patronage of Queen Caroline, who seems to have settled him at Windsor, and he became a clergyman in 1746. But he suffered from depression apparently, and we last hear of him when he drowned himself outside the *Black Lion* inn in Reading 'in a fit of despondency.'

THOMAS HARDY (1840–1928)

The connections of the novelist and poet Thomas Hardy with Reading are slight, but of some literary interest. Although the Dorset writer may only have visited Reading once in 1896, when he was on a journey stretching from Malvern to Dover, Reading features in Hardy's works under the name of Aldbrickham. It always appears on the map of 'The Wessex of the Novels,' just south of 'Castle Royal' (i.e. Windsor), which is found in most editions of Hardy's work, and it is referred to as 'the thriving county-town' in *Life's Little Ironies* of 1894. But Aldbrickham features most notably in *Jude the Obscure* of 1896, when Jude and Sue, though unmarried, are living together in Spring Street, which is almost out in the country, we are told. The day they plan to marry is chilly and damp, with a fog blowing through the town from 'Royal-tower'd Thames,' and they decide not to go through with the ceremony, and when Jude loses his job because of his unconventional relationship with Sue, they are forced to leave Aldbrickham.

Just a few miles from Reading the poet Alfred (later Lord) Tennyson (1809–1892) met and married Emily Sellwood in the village of Shiplake in 1850. The ceremony was performed by the Rev. Robert Rawnsley, the Vicar of Shiplake, an old friend of both wife and groom. Some readers claim that parts of Tennyson's great poem *In Memoriam* were composed during one of Tennyson's pre-wedding visits. George Orwell (1903–1950) also lived at Shiplake in his youth – from 1912–1915 at Rose Lawn in Station Road – before achieving fame for such books as *Animal Farm* (1945). Lytton Strachey (1880–1932), the biographer and critic, lived at nearby Tidmarsh in the last years of his life.

J. K. JEROME (1859–1927)

J. K. Jerome, the novelist and dramatist, also had some knowledge of Reading. He often enjoyed boating, and actually spent his honeymoon on the Thames. His enormously popular humorous novel *Three Men in a Boat* (1889) focuses on our great river and its environment, of course, but Jerome did not seem too impressed. 'The river is dirty and dismal here,' he says. 'One does not linger in the neighbourhood of Reading.'

W. H. HUDSON (1841–1922)

W. H. Hudson, the Argentine-born naturalist and novelist, was equally unimpressed, referring to Reading in *Afoot in England* (1909) as 'the hated biscuit metropolis.' Brought up in the open spaces of Argentina, Hudson hated most towns and cities, but he did enjoy the wooded countryside around Aldermaston and Silchester, however. 'It has long been one of my favourite haunts, summer and winter,' he says.

THE TWO LAWRENCES

The two Lawrences also have connections with Reading, by coincidence in the same year of 1919.

D. H. Lawrence (1885–1930), the novelist and poet, lived at Chapel Cottage in Hermitage, near Newbury, in 1918, and he also stayed for a time at a friend's house 'The Myrtles' in Pangbourne. But Lawrence was always restless, short of money and often in poor health. In the summer of 1919 he paid a visit to Reading, where, we learn, he bought a melon. Later in the year he decided to leave England for Italy, and where before leaving did he sell his books but in Reading?

The visit of T. E. Lawrence, 'Lawrence of Arabia,' (1888–1935), famous soldier, diplomat and writer, was even more bizarre. At the end of World War I, Lawrence decided to write a history of the Arab Revolt and the part he played in it. By the end of the summer of 1919 he had almost finished it. But just before the end of the year he took the bulk of the manuscript with him in a large bag on the train from London to Oxford. Having to change trains at Reading, he went into the refreshment room, put the bag under his table, and forgot about it when he went to catch his train. As soon as he reached Oxford, he telephoned back to Reading, but the bag had disappeared, and has never been seen again. Helped by his diaries and his photographic memory, however, Lawrence completely re-wrote the missing manuscript by the spring of 1920, and the book was published as *The Seven Pillars of Wisdom* in 1926.

Two mysteries remain, however, as we conclude this brief account of Reading writers. Has anyone in Reading ever seen T. E. Lawrence's missing manuscript? And whatever happened to those second-hand books which were sold by D. H. Lawrence?

ACKNOWLEDGEMENTS

For advice and assistance of various kinds, I am grateful to Martin Andrews,
Michael Bott, Cedric Brown, David Cliffe, John Froy, Andrew Gurr, Lionel
Kelly, David Knott, Christopher Salvesen, Bill Watts and Michael Twyman.
The most useful printed sources are:

---*A Famous Bookselling Business*. *The Bookseller* (London), 20 January 1911

Andrews, Martin, *The Life and Work of Robert Gibbings*. Bicester: Primrose
Hill, 2003

Bond, Michael, *Bears & Forebears: A Life so Far*, London: HarperCollins, 1996

Brain, John A., *Berkshire Ballads and Other Papers*. Reading: Thomas Thorp,
1904

Butts, Dennis, *Mistress of Our Tears: A Literary, and Bibliographical Study
of Barbara Hofland*. Aldershot: Scolar Press, 1992

Cooper, John James, *Some Worthies of Reading*. London: Swarthmore Press,
1923

Dearing, John, *Some Hymn Writers Connected with Reading*. Reading:
St. Mary's Castle Street, 2004

Dickens, Charles, *The Letters of Charles Dickens*, edited by Madeline House,
Graham Storey et al., 12 vols. Oxford: The Clarendon Press, 1965–2002

Dormer, Ernest W., *Gray of Reading: A Sixteenth Century Controversialist and Ballad-writer.* Reading: Bradley & Son, 1923

Ellmann, Richard, *Oscar Wilde.* London: Hamish Hamilton, 1987

Grove, Valerie, *Laurie Lee: The Well Loved Stranger.* London: Viking, 1999

Hart, B.H. Liddell, *'T.E. Lawrence': in Arabia and After.* London: Cape, 1934

Holt, J.C., *The University of Reading: the first fifty years.* Reading: Reading University Press, 1977

Holmes, Richard, *Coleridge: Early Visions.* London: Hodder & Stoughton, 1989

Lawrence, D.H., *A Composite Biography*, edited by E.Nehls. Madison: University of Wisconsin, 3 vols., 1957–1959

Mack, Maynard, *Alexander Pope.* New Haven: Yale University Press, 1985

Stallworthy, J., *Wilfred Owen.* London: O.U.P. and Chatto and Windus, 1974

Watson, Vera, *Mary Russell Mitford.* London: Evans, n.d.

Welsh, Charles, *A Bookseller of the Last Century: Being Some Account of the Life of John Newbery ...* [1885]. New Jersey: Augustus Kelley, 1972